MOVIE FAVORITES

FOR HARMONICA

ARRANGED BY BOBBY JOE HOLMAN

CONTENTS

TIP BOX
To play all the music in this book,
try Bobby Joe's "BAG-OF-HARPS."
To purchase, contact:
Musicians Boulevard
2511 E. Thousand Oaks Blvd.
Thousand Oaks, CA 91362
Tel (805) 494-4683
Fax (805) 497-1386

ISBN 0-634-01674-1

HAL•LEONARD®
CORPORATION
7777 W. BLUEMOUND RD. P.O. BOX 13819 MILWAUKEE, WI 53213

T0052791

How to Use the Music in This Book

This book is part of an ongoing series of themed publications covering a wide variety of musical styles. Each one provides a selection of the most popular and requested songs arranged for both the diatonic and chromatic harmonicas.

To understand the techniques required to play the songs presented, it is recommended that you thoroughly study both of my harmonica instruction books: The Hal Leonard Complete Harmonica Method—Book One—The Diatonic Harmonica, and The Hal Leonard Complete Harmonica Method—Book Two—The Chromatic Harmonica

Understanding this system will enable you to fully enjoy the musical treasures found within.

Heart to Harp,

Bobby Joe Holman

Understanding Harmonica Tablature for the Diatonic Harmonica

Before attempting to play the songs in this book, make sure you understand each harmonica tablature symbol, shown below. Understanding these symbols and reading the information on each song will enable you to learn and play these songs more easily and quickly.

To understand how to bend notes and which notes can be bent on a diatonic harmonica, refer to The Hal Leonard Complete Harmonica Method–Book One–The Diatonica Harmonica, Chapter 1. The diatonic harmonica, due to design limitations, requires this many symbols.

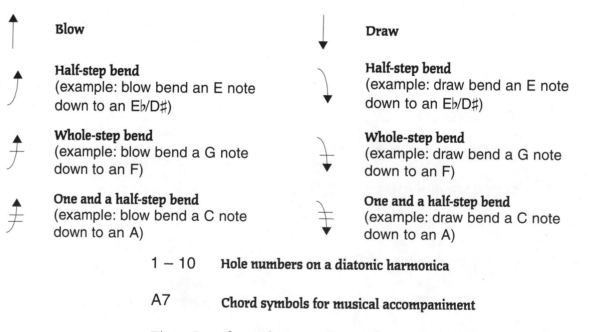

Blow

Half-step bend
(example: blow bend an E note down to an E♭/D♯)

Whole-step bend
(example: blow bend a G note down to an F)

One and a half-step bend
(example: blow bend a C note down to an A)

Draw

Half-step bend
(example: draw bend an E note down to an E♭/D♯)

Whole-step bend
(example: draw bend a G note down to an F)

One and a half-step bend
(example: draw bend a C note down to an A)

1 – 10 Hole numbers on a diatonic harmonica

A7 Chord symbols for musical accompaniment

E♭ to C Change from one diatonic harmonica to another in a different key

Born Free
from the Columbia Pictures' Release BORN FREE
Words by Don Black
Music by John Barry

Key: F
Harmonica: F

Alfie
Theme from the Paramount Picture ALFIE
Words by Hal David
Music by Burt Bacharach

Key: C
Harmonica: C

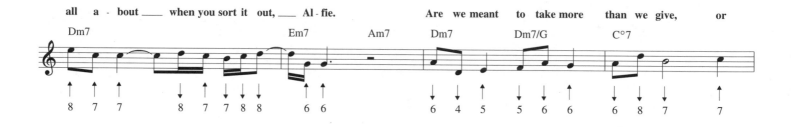

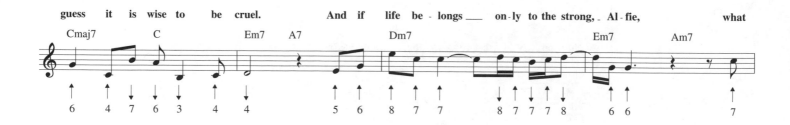

Bless the Beasts and Children

from BLESS THE BEASTS AND CHILDREN

Words and Music by Barry DeVorzon and Perry Botkin, Jr.

Key: B♭

Harmonica: B♭, E♭, D♭

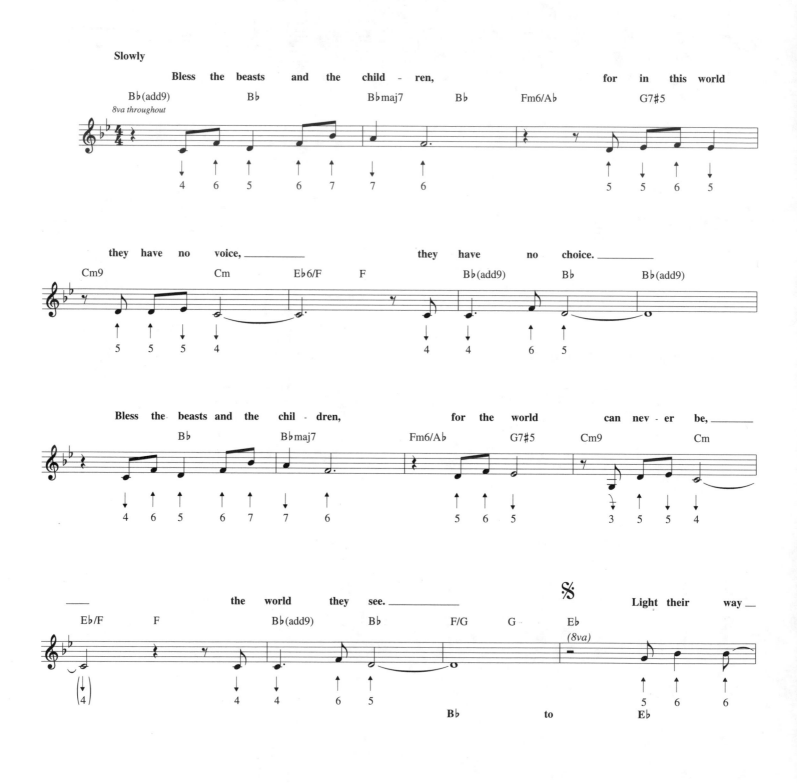

Georgy Girl
from GEORGY GIRL
Words by Jim Dale
Music by Tom Springfield

Key: E♭
Harmonica: E♭

9

Maybe This Time
from the Musical CABARET
Lyric by Fred Ebb
Music by John Kander

Key: C
Harmonica: C

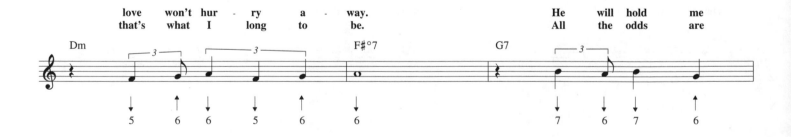

Midnight Cowboy
from the Motion Picture MIDNIGHT COWBOY
Music by John Barry
Lyric by Jack Gold

Key: C
Harmonica: C

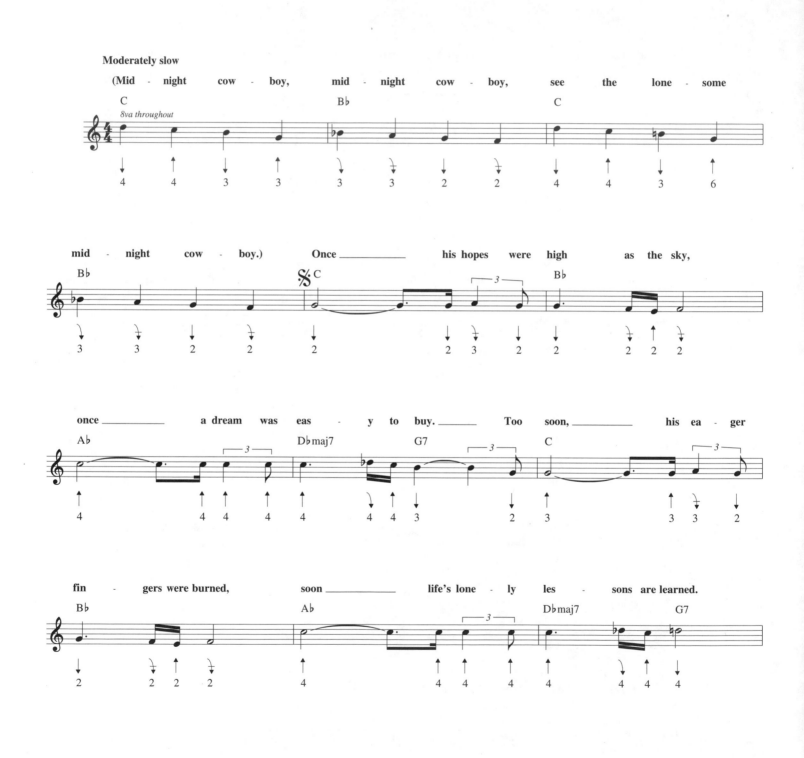

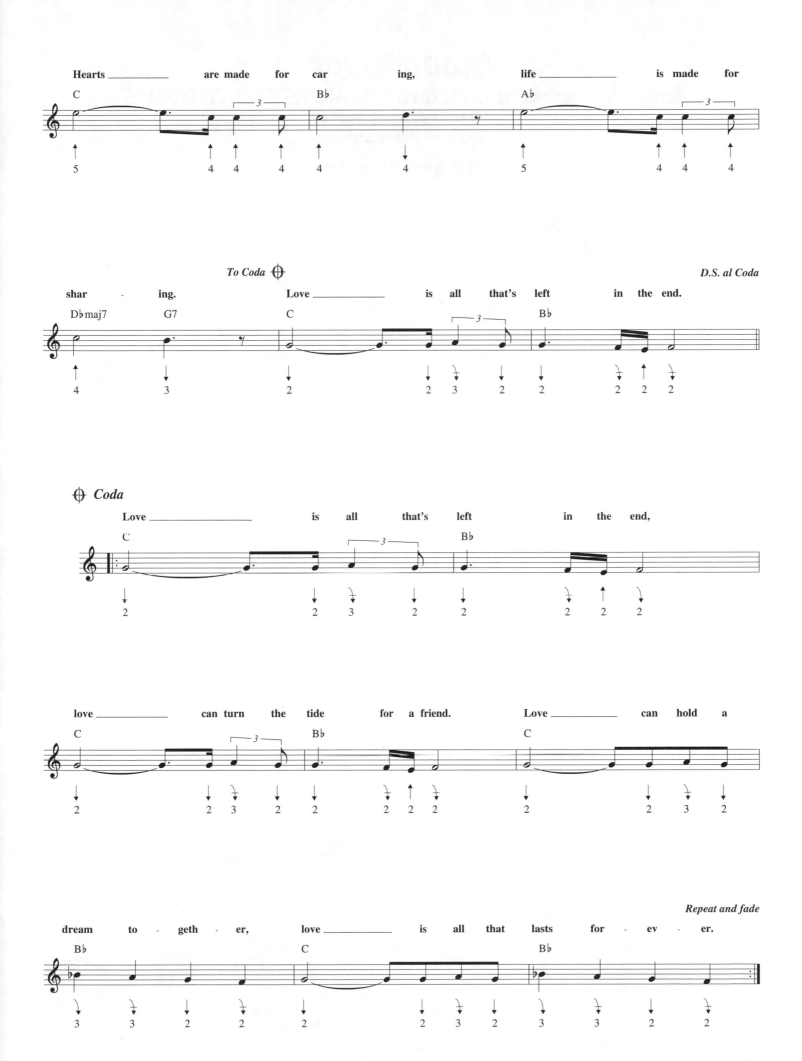

Moon River

from the Paramount Picture BREAKFAST AT TIFFANY'S

Words by Johnny Mercer
Music by Henry Mancini

Key: C
Harmonica: C

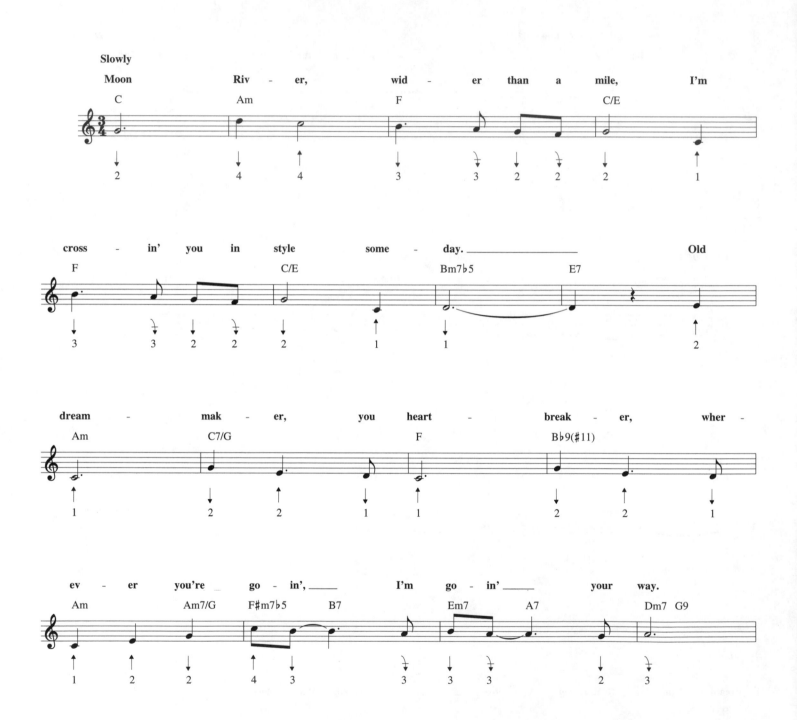

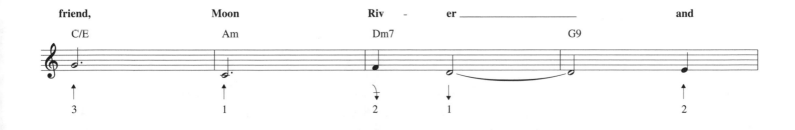

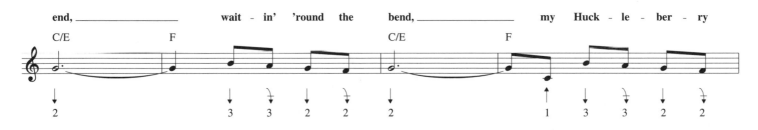

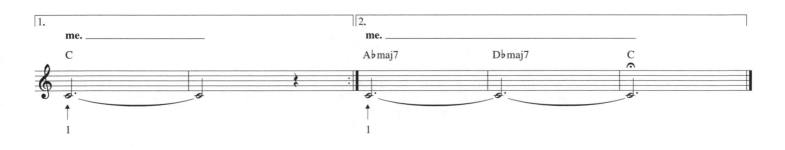

Picnic
from the Columbia Technicolor Picture PICNIC
Words by Steve Allen
Music by George W. Duning

Key: C
Harmonica: C

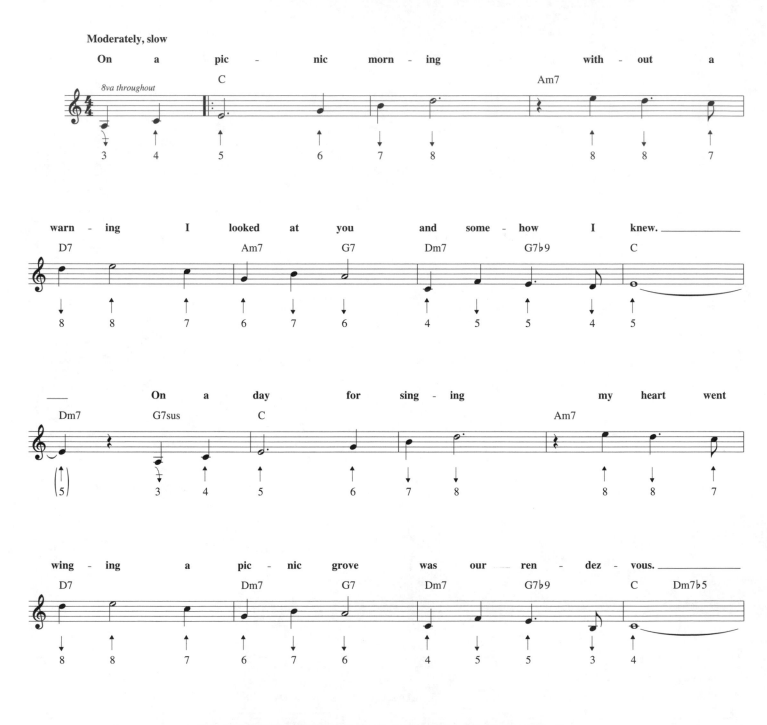

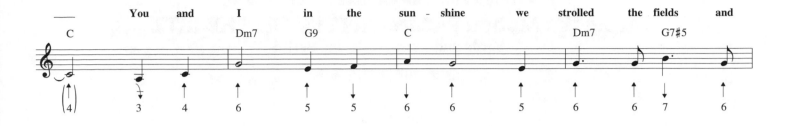

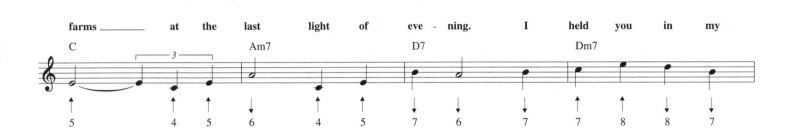

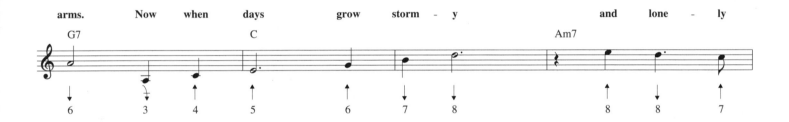

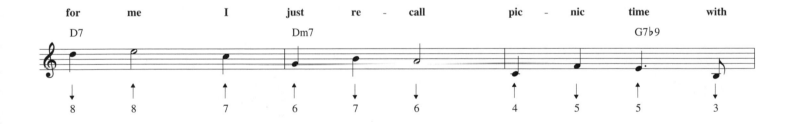

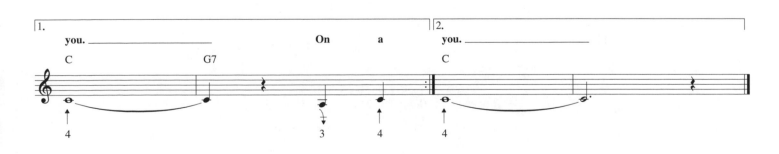

Puttin' On the Ritz
from the Motion Picture PUTTIN' ON THE RITZ
Words and Music by Irving Berlin

Key: A♭

Harmonica: A♭

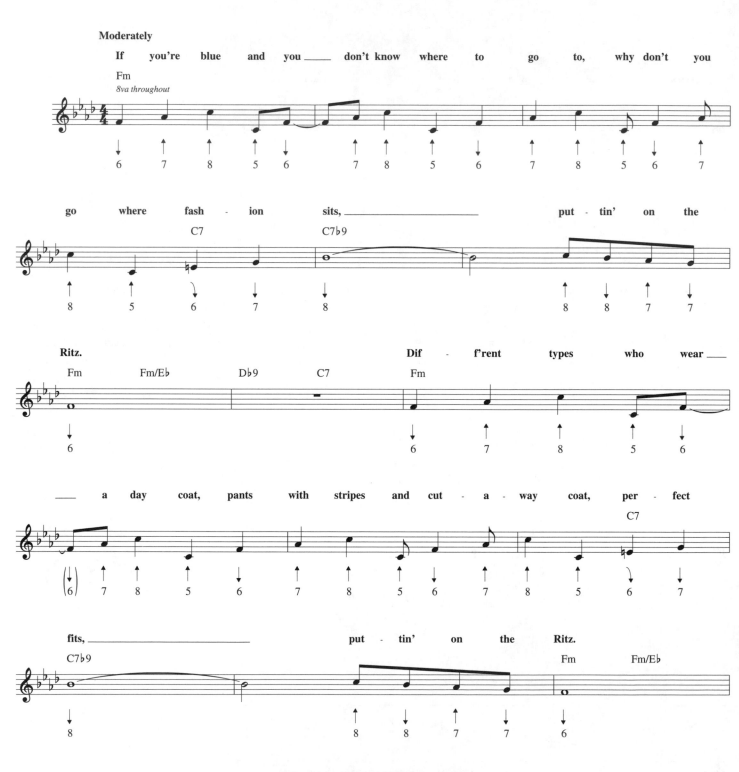

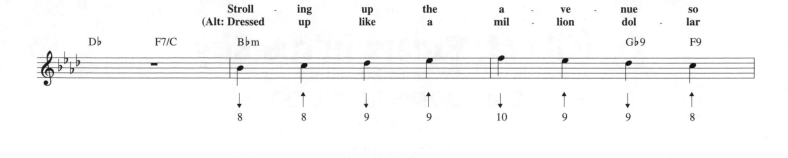

Stroll - ing up the a - ve - nue so
(Alt: Dressed up like a mil - lion dol - lar

Db   F7/C   Bbm   Gb9   F9

8   8   9   9   10   9   9   8

hap - py. _____   All dressed up just
troup - er. _____   Try - ing hard just to

Bbm6   Eb9 Eb7#5 Eb7   Ab6   Fm7

8   8   7   8   8   9

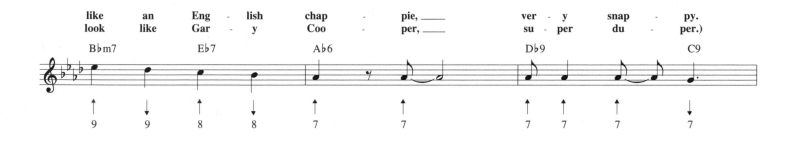

like an Eng - lish chap - pie, _____   ver - y snap - py.
look like Gar - y Coo - per, _____   su - per du - per.)

Bbm7   Eb7   Ab6   Db9   C9

9   9   8   8   7   7   7   7   7   7

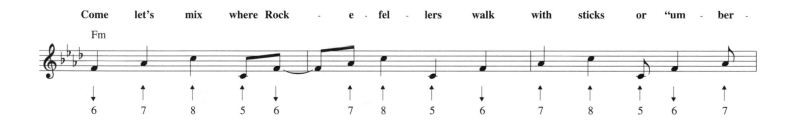

Come let's mix where Rock - e - fel - lers walk with sticks or "um - ber -

Fm

6   7   8   5   6   7   8   5   6   7   8   5   6   7

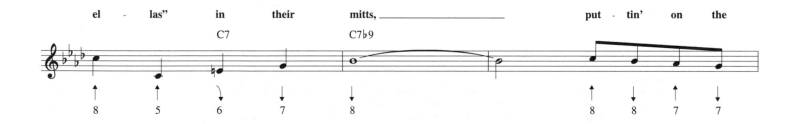

el - las" in their mitts, _____ put - tin' on the

C7   C7b9

8   5   6   7   8   8   8   7   7

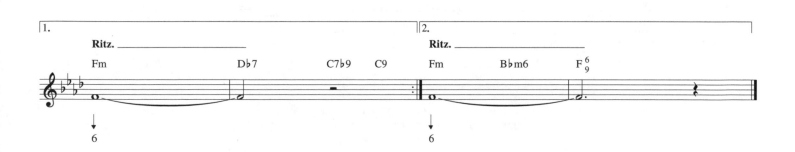

1.   2.
Ritz. _____   Ritz. _____

Fm   Db7   C7b9 C9   Fm   Bbm6   F 6/9

6   6

(Ghost) Riders in the Sky
(A Cowboy Legend)
from RIDERS IN THE SKY
By Stan Jones

Key: B♭
Harmonica: B♭

Chim Chim Cher-ee

from Walt Disney's MARY POPPINS

Words and Music by Richard M. Sherman and Robert B. Sherman

Key: E♭
Harmonica: E♭

23

Speak Softly, Love
(Love Theme)
from the Paramount Picture THE GODFATHER

Words by Larry Kusik
Music by Nino Rota

Key: E♭
Harmonica: E♭

Stormy Weather
(Keeps Rainin' All the Time)
featured in the Motion Picture STORMY WEATHER
Lyric by Ted Koehler
Music by Harold Arlen

Key: G
Harmonica: G

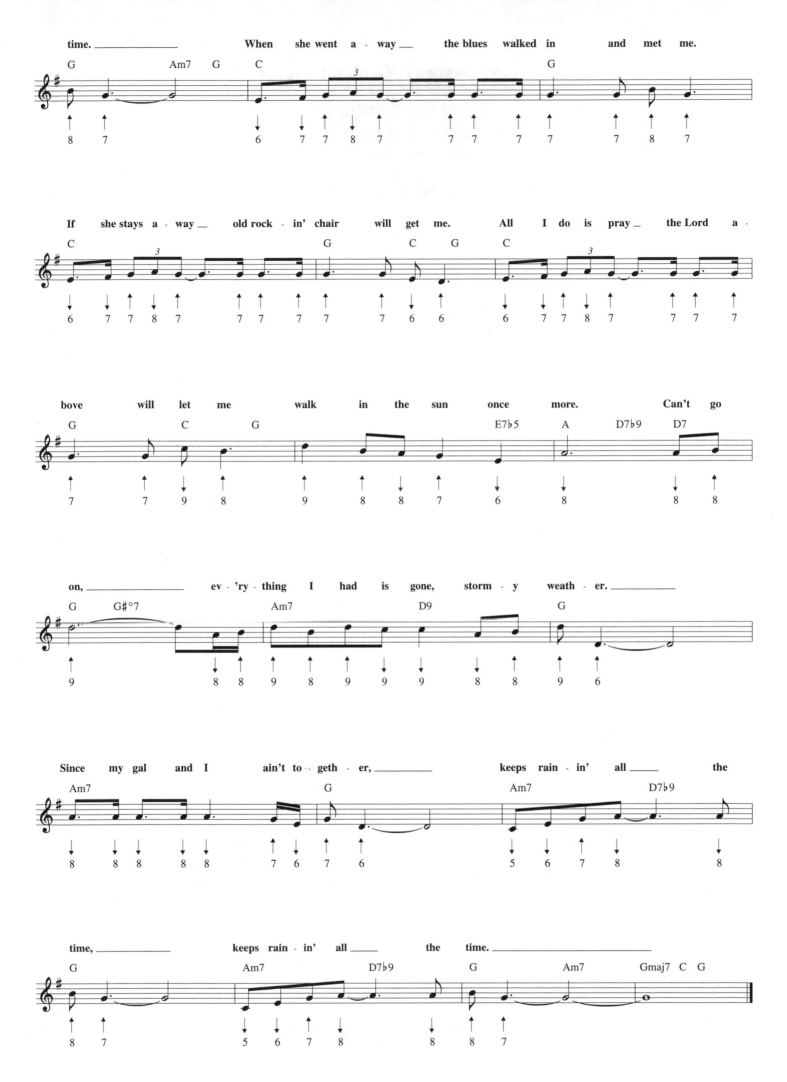

Tenderly
from TORCH SONG
Lyric by Jack Lawrence
Music by Walter Gross

Key: E♭
Harmonica: E♭

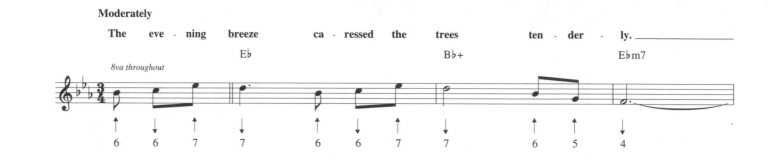

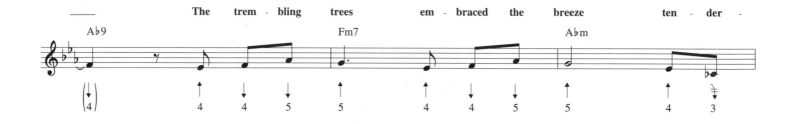

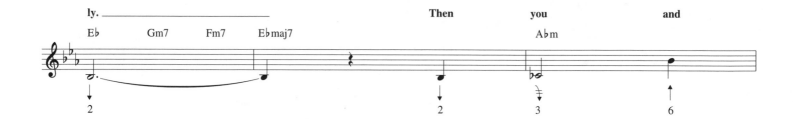

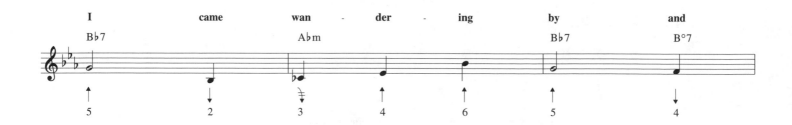

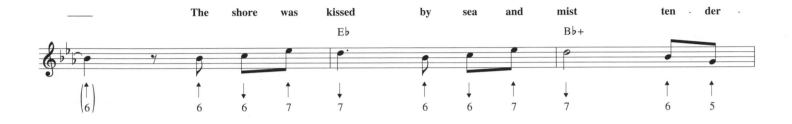

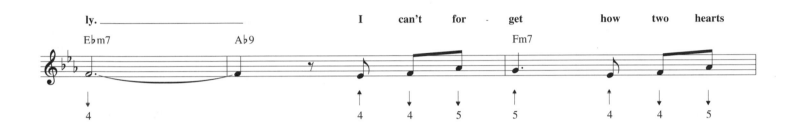

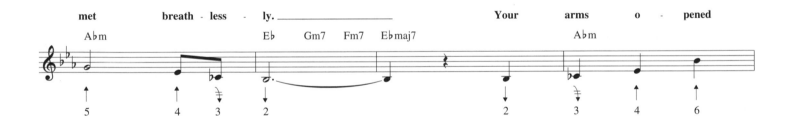

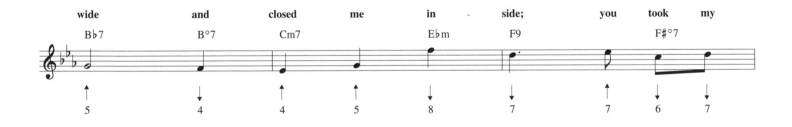

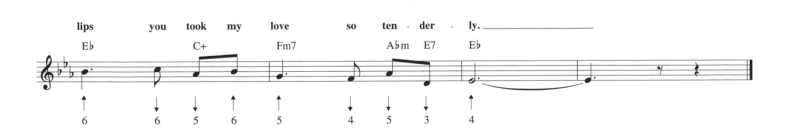

A Time for Us
(Love Theme)
from the Paramount Picture ROMEO AND JULIET
Words by Larry Kusik and Eddie Snyder
Music by Nino Rota

Key: B♭
Harmonica: B♭

What a Wonderful World
featured in the Motion Picture GOOD MORNING VIETNAM
Words and Music by George David Weiss and Bob Thiele

Key: F
Harmonica: F

Unchained Melody
from the Motion Picture UNCHAINED
featured in the Motion Picture GHOST

Lyric by Hy Zaret
Music by Alex North

Key: G
Harmonica: G

Zip-A-Dee-Doo-Dah

from Walt Disney's SONG OF THE SOUTH

Words by Ray Gilbert
Music by Allie Wrubel

Key: Bb
Harmonica: Bb

Understanding Harmonica Tablature for the Chromatic Harmonica

Before attempting to play the songs in this section, the same approach is required to play these songs as in the diatonic section of this book. Make sure you understand each harmonica tablature symbol shown below to expedite the learning process.

Unlike the diatonic harmonica, the chromatic harmonica was designed to play every note in a two-octave scale (Hohner Chrometta #250), two and a half-octave scale (Hohner Chromatica #260), three-octave scale (Hohner Super Chromatica #270 or Chrometta #255) or four-octave scale (Hohner Super 64 #280). There are no bent notes required or changing of keys when playing this music on a chromatic harmonica.

To understand how to play this music on the chromatic harmonica, you should refer to The Hal Leonard Complete Harmonica Method – Book Two – The Chromatic Harmonica.

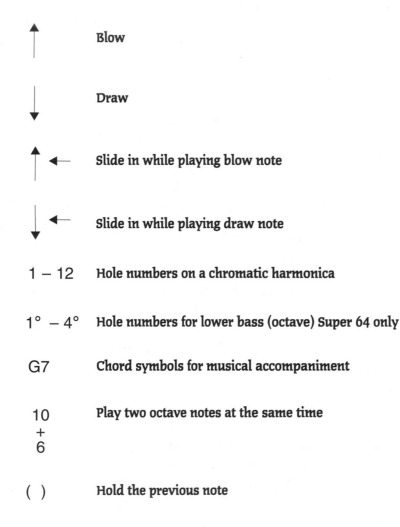

↑	Blow
↓	Draw
↑ ←	Slide in while playing blow note
↓ ←	Slide in while playing draw note
1 – 12	Hole numbers on a chromatic harmonica
1° – 4°	Hole numbers for lower bass (octave) Super 64 only
G7	Chord symbols for musical accompaniment
10 + 6	Play two octave notes at the same time
( )	Hold the previous note

Born Free
from the Columbia Pictures' Release BORN FREE
Words by Don Black
Music by John Barry

Key: F
Harmonica: All chromatic harmonicas

Alfie
Theme from the Paramount Picture ALFIE
Words by Hal David
Music by Burt Bacharach

Key: Eb
Harmonica: Hohner Super 64 only

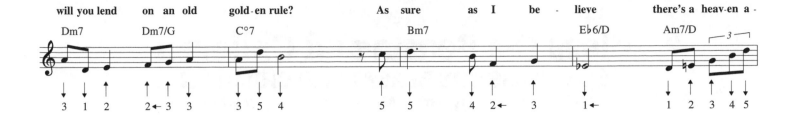

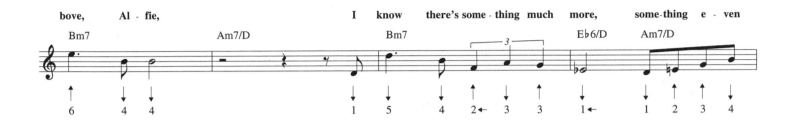

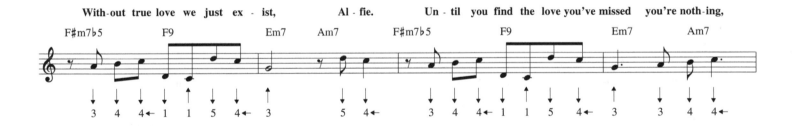

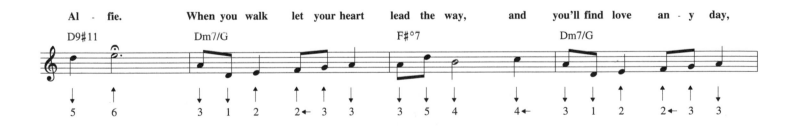

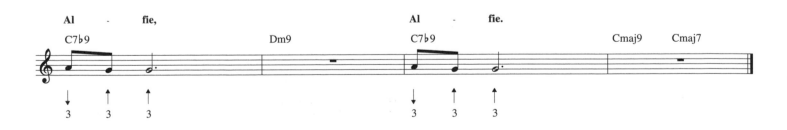

Bless the Beasts and Children

from BLESS THE BEASTS AND CHILDREN

Words and Music by Barry DeVorzon and Perry Botkin, Jr.

Key: B♭

Harmonica: All chromatic harmonicas

The Entertainer
featured in the Motion Picture THE STING
By Scott Joplin

Key: C
Harmonica: All chromatic harmonicas

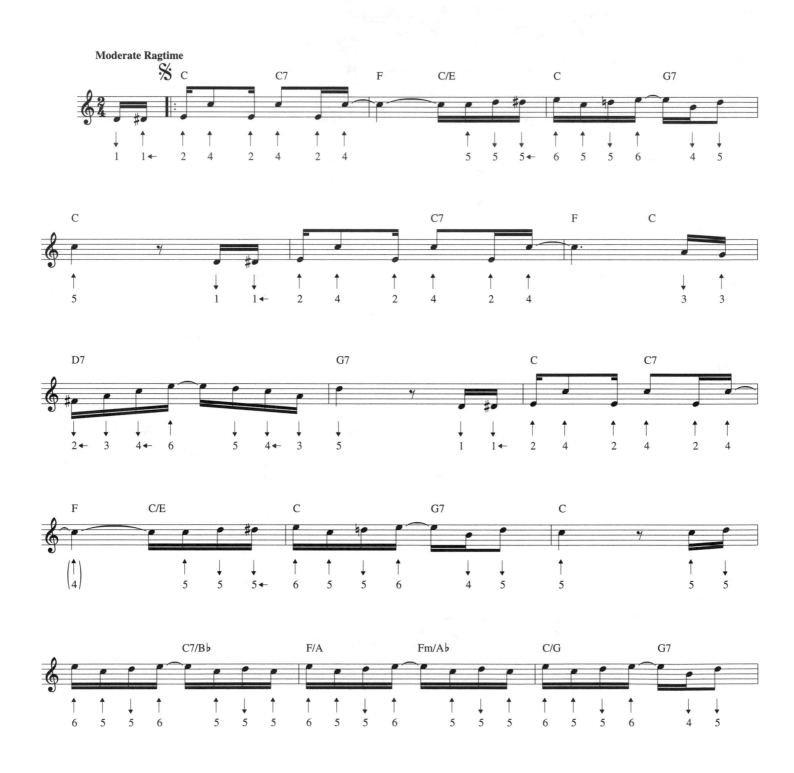

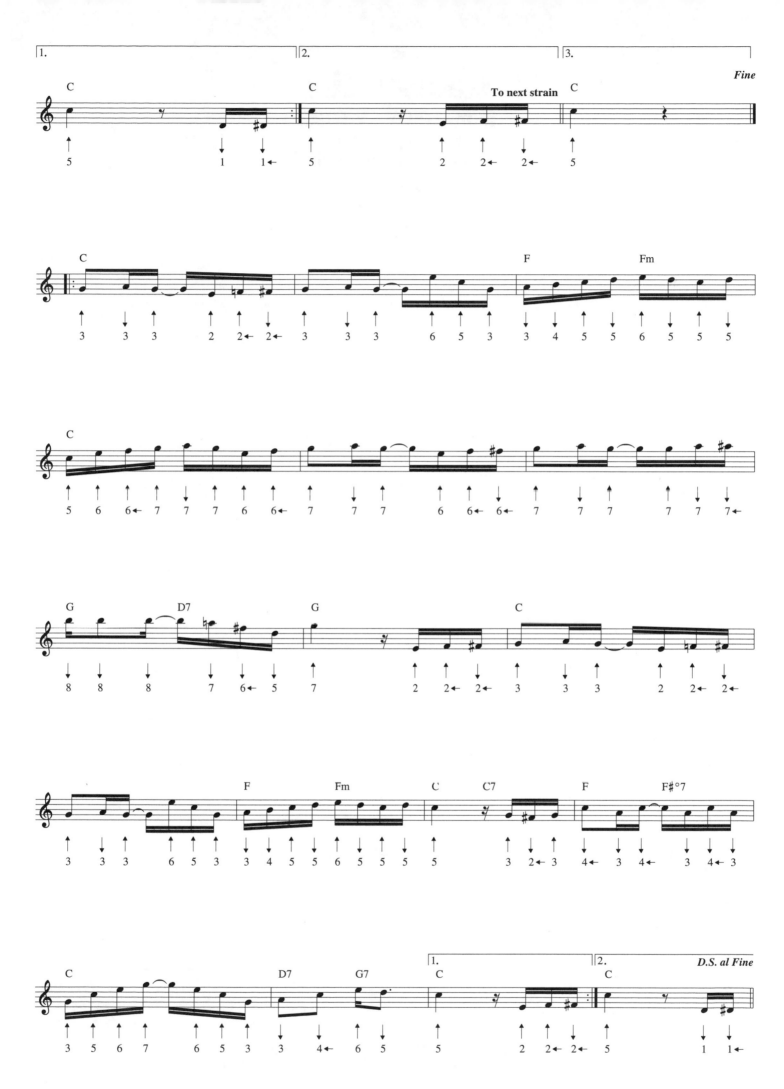

Georgy Girl
from GEORGY GIRL
Words by Jim Dale
Music by Tom Springfield

Key: E♭
Harmonica: Hohner Super 64 only

45

Maybe This Time
from the Musical CABARET
Lyric by Fred Ebb
Music by John Kander

Key: C
Harmonica: Hohner Super 64 only

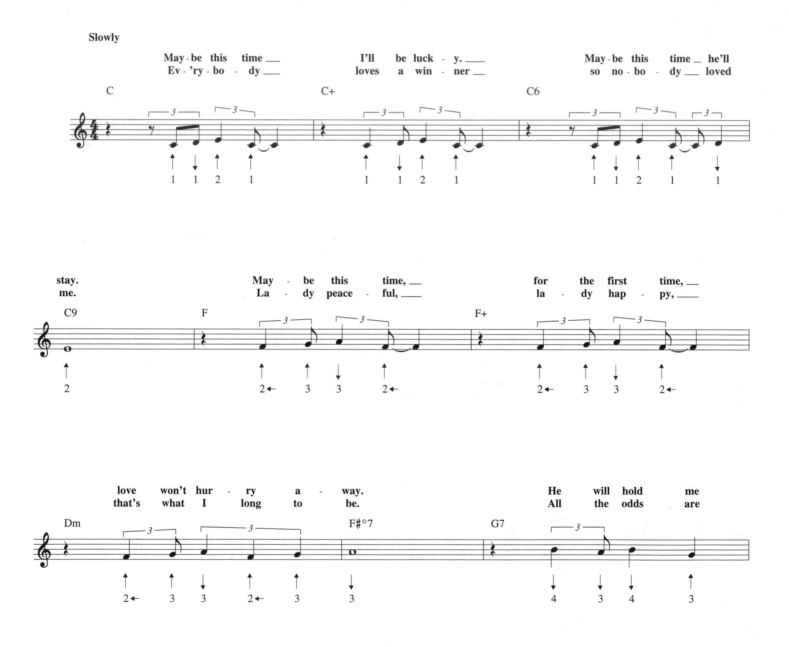

Midnight Cowboy
from the Motion Picture MIDNIGHT COWBOY

Music by John Barry
Lyric by Jack Gold

Key: C
Harmonica: All chromatic harmonicas

49

Moon River

from the Paramount Picture BREAKFAST AT TIFFANY'S

Words by Johnny Mercer
Music by Henry Mancini

Key: C
Harmonica: All chromatic harmonicas

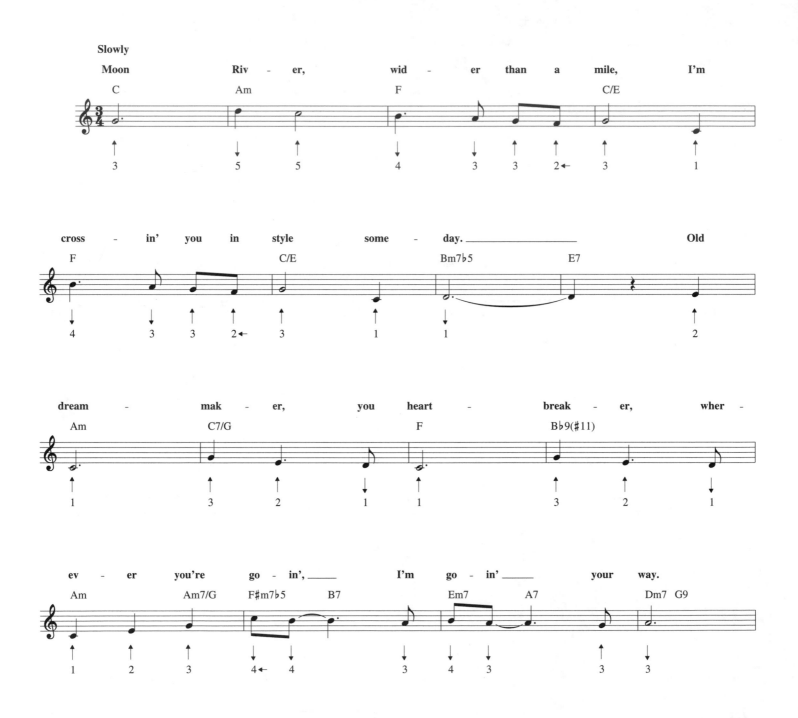

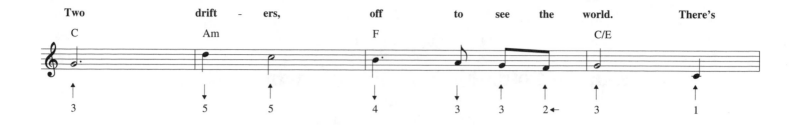

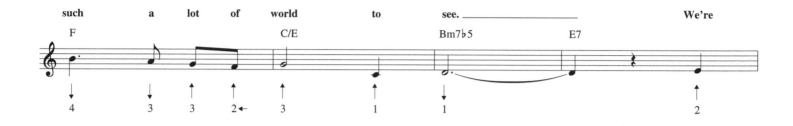

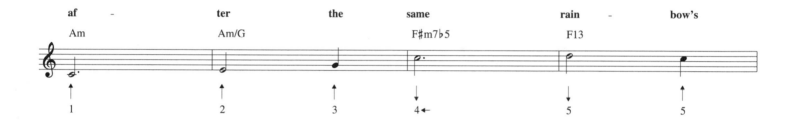

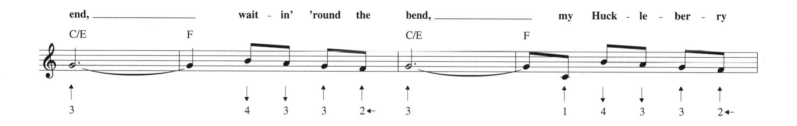

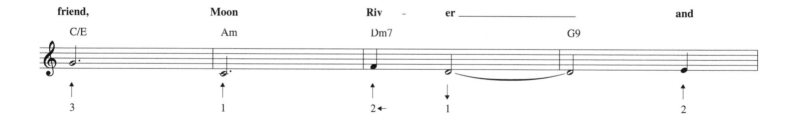

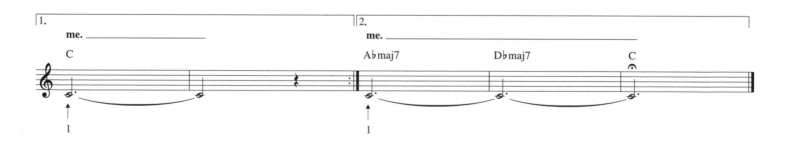

Picnic
from the Columbia Technicolor Picture PICNIC
Words by Steve Allen
Music by George W. Duning

Key: C
Harmonica: Hohner Super 64 only

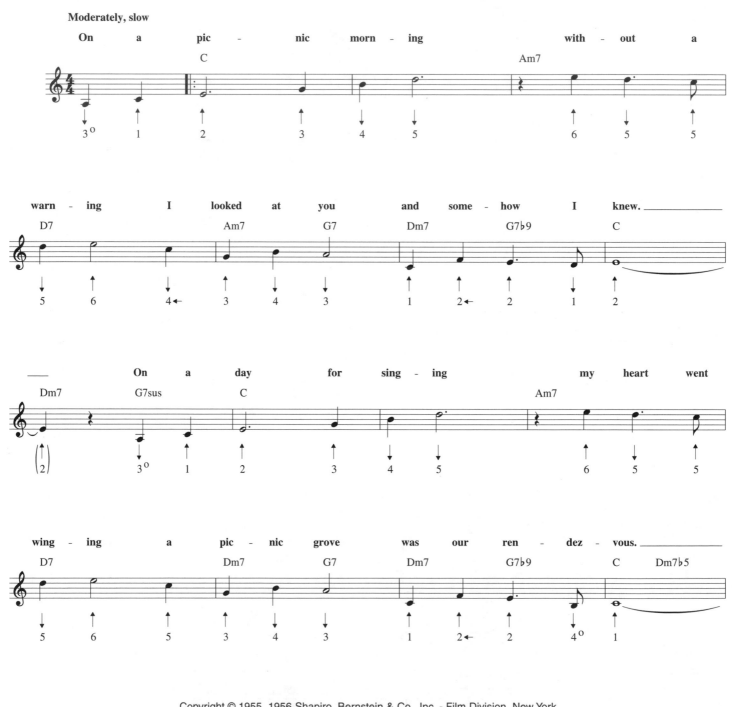

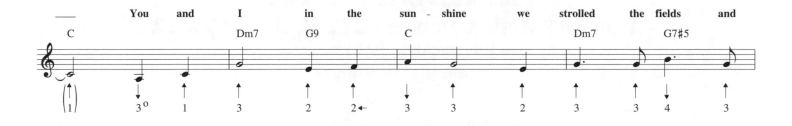

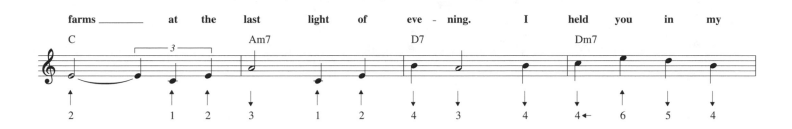

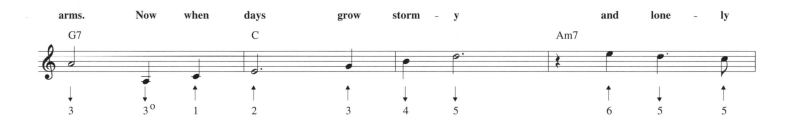

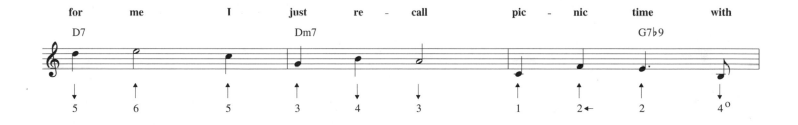

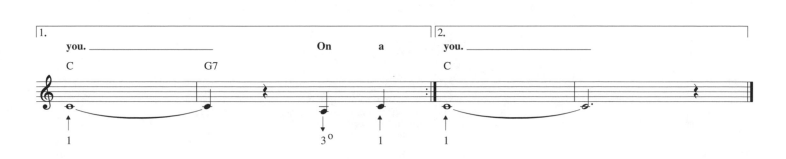

Puttin' On the Ritz
from the Motion Picture PUTTIN' ON THE RITZ
Words and Music by Irving Berlin

Key: Ab
Harmonica: All chromatic harmonicas

(Ghost) Riders in the Sky
(A Cowboy Legend)
from RIDERS IN THE SKY
By Stan Jones

Key: B♭
Harmonica: Hohner Super 64 only

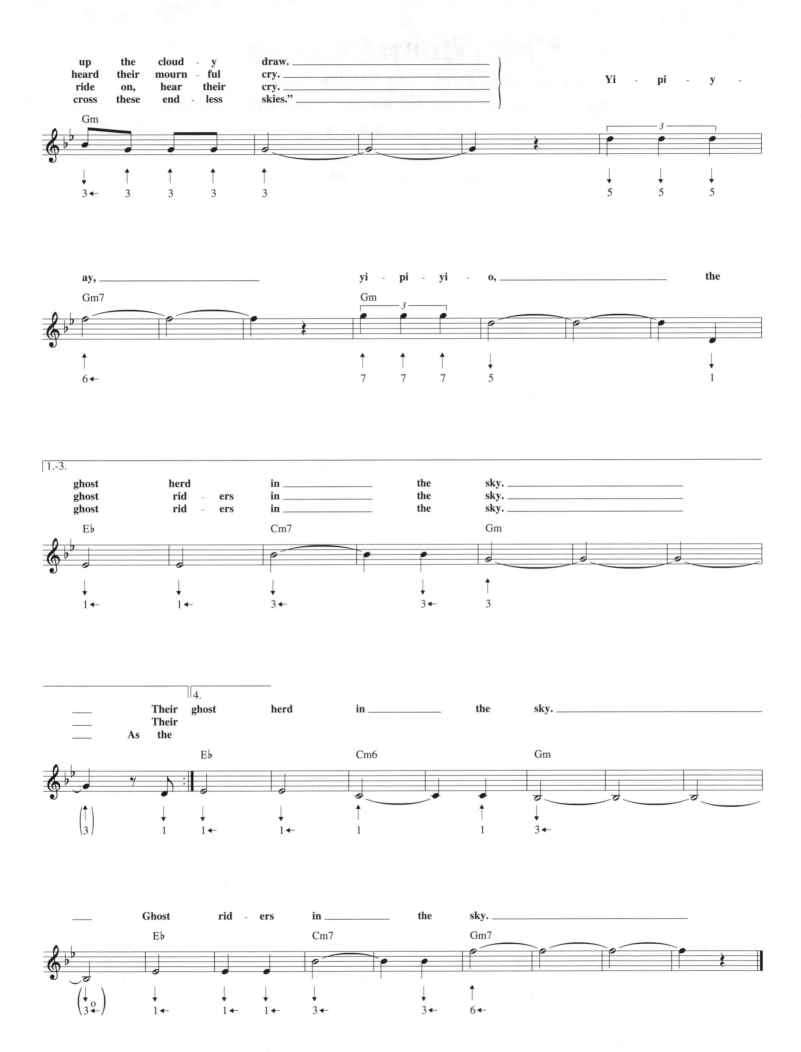

Chim Chim Cher-ee
from Walt Disney's MARY POPPINS
Words and Music by Richard M. Sherman and Robert B. Sherman

Key: E♭
Harmonica: All chromatic harmonicas

Speak Softly, Love

(Love Theme)
from the Paramount Picture THE GODFATHER

Words by Larry Kusik
Music by Nino Rota

Key: E♭
Harmonica: Hohner Super 64 only

Stormy Weather

(Keeps Rainin' All the Time)

featured in the Motion Picture STORMY WEATHER

Lyric by Ted Koehler
Music by Harold Arlen

Key: G
Harmonica: All chromatic harmonicas

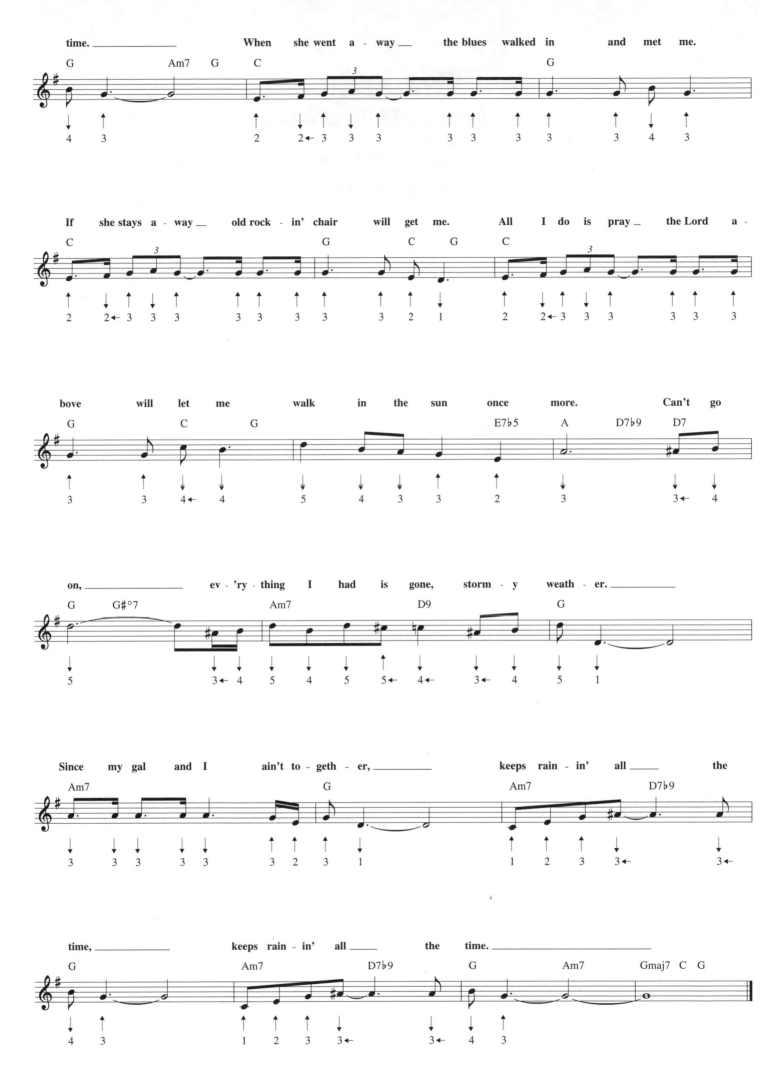

Tenderly
from TORCH SONG

Lyric by Jack Lawrence
Music by Walter Gross

Key: E♭
Harmonica: Hohner Super 64 only

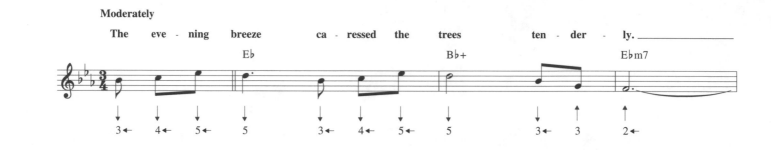

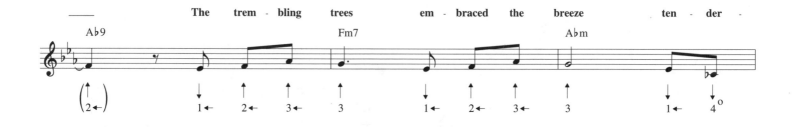

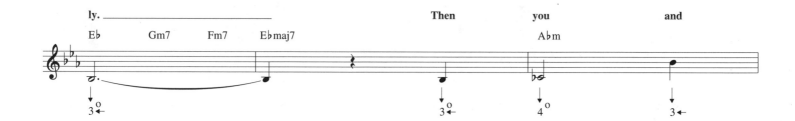

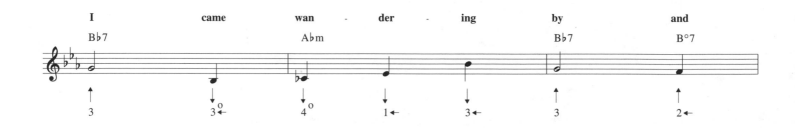

A Time for Us

(Love Theme)

from the Paramount Picture ROMEO AND JULIET

Words by Larry Kusik and Eddie Snyder
Music by Nino Rota

Key: B♭
Harmonica: Hohner Super 64 only

What a Wonderful World
featured in the Motion Picture GOOD MORNING VIETNAM
Words and Music by George David Weiss and Bob Thiele

Key: F
Harmonica: All chromatic harmonicas

Unchained Melody

from the Motion Picture UNCHAINED
featured in the Motion Picture GHOST

Lyric by Hy Zaret
Music by Alex North

Key: G
Harmonica: Hohner Super 64 only

Zip-A-Dee-Doo-Dah
from Walt Disney's SONG OF THE SOUTH

Words by Ray Gilbert
Music by Allie Wrubel

Key: Bb
Harmonica: Hohner Super 64 only

HAL LEONARD PRESENTS EIGHT GREAT HARMONICA BOOKS!

THE HAL LEONARD COMPLETE HARMONICA METHOD – THE DIATONIC HARMONICA
Bobby Joe Holman
The only harmonica method specific to the diatonic harmonica, covering all six positions. This book/CD pack contains 29 songs and musical examples that take beginners from the basics on through to the most advanced techniques available for the contemporary harmonica player. Each section contains appropriate songs and exercises (which are demonstrated on the CD) that enable the player to quickly learn the various concepts presented. Every aspect of this versatile musical instrument is explored and explained in easy-to-understand detail with illustrations. The musical styles include traditional, blues, pop and rock.
00841285 Book/CD Pack $12.95

THE HAL LEONARD COMPLETE HARMONICA METHOD – THE CHROMATIC HARMONICA
Bobby Joe Holman
The only harmonica method to present the chromatic harmonica in 14 scales and modes in all 12 keys! This book/CD pack will take beginners from the basics on through to the most advanced techniques available for the contemporary harmonica player. Each section contains appropriate songs and exercises (which are demonstrated on the CD) that enable the player to quickly learn the various concepts presented. Every aspect of this versatile musical instrument is explored and explained in easy-to-understand detail with illustrations. The musical styles include traditional, blues, pop and rock.
00841286 Book/CD Pack $12.95

BROADWAY SONGS
19 show-stopping Broadway tunes for the harmonica. Songs include: Ain't Misbehavin' • Bali Ha'i • Blue Skies • Camelot • Caravan • Climb Ev'ry Mountain • Do-Re-Mi • Edelweiss • Give My Regards to Broadway • Gonna Build a Mountain • Hello, Dolly! • Hello, Young Lovers • I've Grown Accustomed to Her Face • The Impossible Dream (The Quest) • Masquerade • Memory • Oklahoma • On a Clear Day (You Can See Forever) • People.
00820009 $8.95

CHRISTMAS CAROLS AND HYMNS
19 songs, including Auld Lang Syne • Deck the Hall • The First Noel • It Came Upon the Midnight Clear • Jingle Bells • Joy to the World • Silent Night • We Wish You a Merry Christmas • and more.
00820008 $8.95

CLASSICAL FAVORITES
18 classical treasures, including: By the Beautiful Blue Danube • Clair De Lune • The Flight of the Bumble Bee • Gypsy Rondo • Two-Part Invention in C Major • Lascia Ch'io Pianga • Minuet (from Don Giovanni) • Minuet in G Major, K. 1 • Piano Sonata No. 14 in C# Minor ("Moonlight") Op. 27 No. 2 First Movement Theme • Symphony No. 6 in F Major ("Pastoral") Third Movement • Prelude in G Minor Op. 23 No. 5 • Surprise Symphony • The Swan (Le Cygne) • Theme from Swan Lake • Symphony No. 5 in C Minor, First Movement Excerpt • Symphony No. 9 in D Op. 125 Second Movement Theme • Waltz in C# Minor • Waltz of the Flowers.
00820006 $7.95

MOVIE FAVORITES
19 songs from the silver screen. Includes: Alfie • Bless the Beasts and Children • Chim Chim Cher-ee • The Entertainer • Georgy Girl • Maybe This Time • Midnight Cowboy • Moon River • Theme from "Picnic" • Puttin' on the Ritz • (Ghost) Riders in the Sky (A Cowboy Legend) • Speak Softly, Love (Love Theme) • Stormy Weather (Keeps Rainin' All the Time) • Tenderly • A Time for Us (Love Theme) • Unchained Melody • What a Wonderful World • Zip-A-Dee-Doo-Dah.
00820014 $8.95

POP/ROCK FAVORITES
17 classic hits, including Abraham, Martin and John • All I Have to Do Is Dream • Blueberry Hill • Copacabana (At the Copa) • Daydream • Green Green Grass of Home • Hanky Panky • Happy Together • Oh, Pretty Woman • Runaway • Sixteen Candles • Sleepwalk • Something • Stand By Me • Tears on My Pillow • Tell It Like It Is • Yakety Yak.
00820013 $8.95

TV FAVORITES
More than 20 couch potato hits. Includes: The Ballad of Davy Crockett • Theme from "Beauty and the Beast" • Theme from "Bewitched" • The Brady Bunch • Brandenburg Concerto No. 2 • Bubbles in the Wine • Call to Glory • Danny Boy (Londonderry Air) • Father Knows Best Theme • Hands of Time • Happy Days • The Little House (On the Prairie) • Mariko Love Theme • Nadia's Theme • Theme from Ninth Symphony • The Odd Couple • Twin Peaks Theme • Theme from "The Untouchables" • Victory at Sea • William Tell Overture • Wings.
00820007 $8.95

0900